Getting dressed for HOLIDAY

STICKER ACTIVITY BOOK

Om KIDZ

An imprint of Om Books International

It's a bright, sunny day and Rosh and Lia are at the beach!

With the stress of school behind, they have all the time to relax on their vacation. Dress them up and let the fun begin!

Ronny and Imee are out on an adventure, camping in the wild.

Take out your stickers and help them set up their campsite.

Polly and Jacob are at the fair. Use stickers to add to their fun.

It's time
for the rides!

Pg-2
Pg-3
Pg-4
FAIR
Pg-6
Pg-5

Pg-7

Pg-8

Pg-9

Pg-10

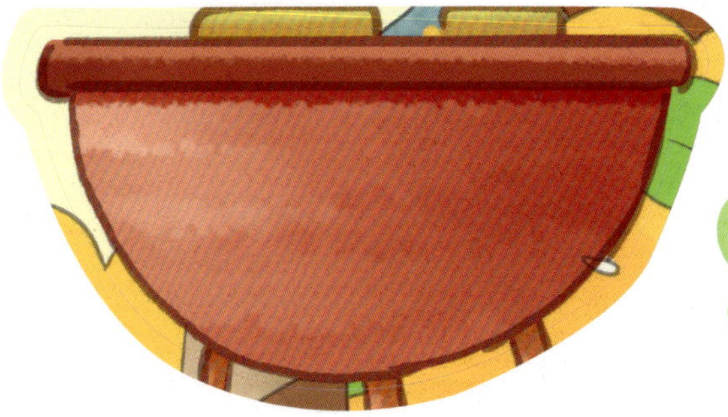

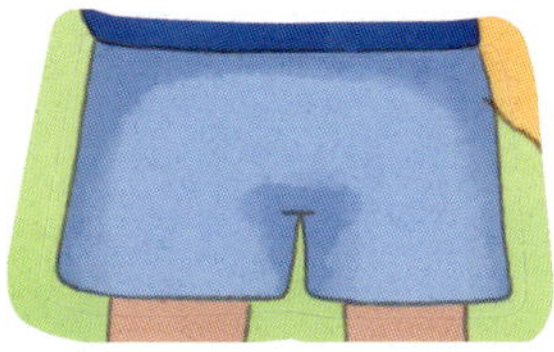

Pg-11

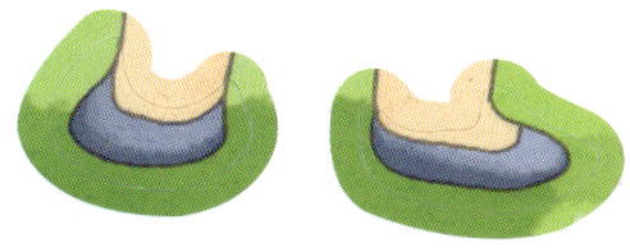
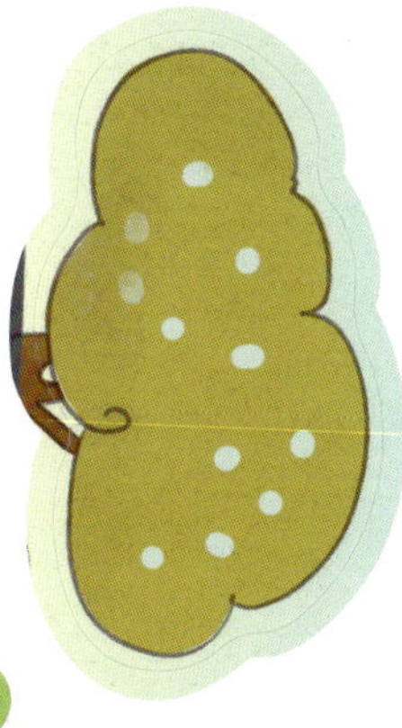

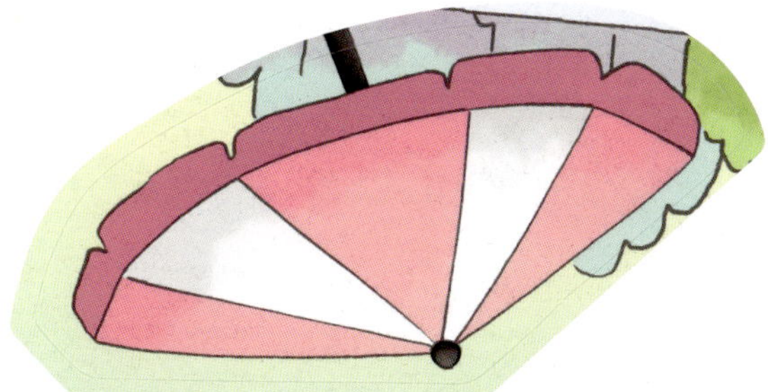

Pg-12

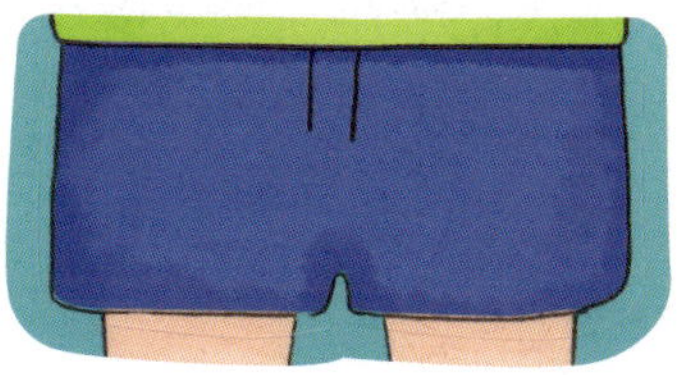
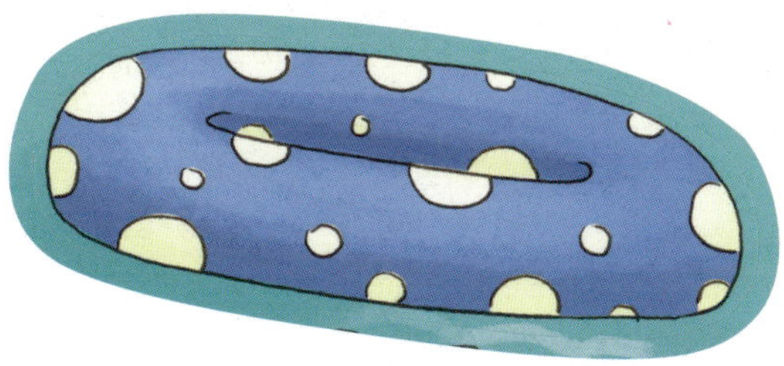

Pg-13

Pg-14

Pg-15

Pg-16

Cock-a-doodle-doo! Kim and Mitty are farmworkers. Help them by using stickers to complete the picture.

It's a Saturday afternoon,
pleasant and lovely.
Mac and Julie
are out for
a picnic.

Let's help them set up by using the stickers!

Swimming on a hot summer day is very fun!

Complete the scene for Jack and Kelly as they go splashing in the water.

Rover and Ellie are on a safari, watching big and small wild animals! Join in their fun and paste some stickers.

Bob is very sporty and loves to ski.
Get him dressed so he can go skiing.